MW00576015

Sasiprapa Muay Thai

Copyright © 2014 by PDC.

All rights reserved.
No part of this publication may be reproduced, distributed, or transmitted in any form or by any means, including photocopying,
recording, or other electronic or mechanical methods, without the prior written permission of the publishers. For permission requests, write to the publishers at the address below.

The PDC Team
5, Beaumont Avenue
Greenbank
Plymouth
Devon UK
PL4 8DX

Ordering Information:
Quantity sales. Special discounts are available on quantity purchases by corporations, associations, and others. For details, contact the authors at the address above.

ISBN 978-0-9571678-6-5

This book has been printed on paper and board certified by the The Forest Stewardship Council® (FSC). This indicates that they are sourced from FSC eco-friendly sustainable sources.

FSC
www.fsc.org
MIX
Paper from
responsible sources
FSC® C006316

Dedications

This book is dedicated to the memory of Chanai Pongsupha.

Thanks to all the fighters, trainers and management at Sasiprapa Gym, Bangkok where the images and trainers notes were exclusively recorded.

Thanks to Mr Aidan Green for proof reading.

Special thanks go to Mr Pongwara Phrommanon, Mr Witthaya Khamlert and Mr Phon Pongjit for demonstrating the techniques.

Sasiprapa Muay Thai

Coaches

You will be able to dip into the book and find inspiration for your Muay Thai classes, sometimes revisiting a forgotten padwork drill, sometimes just reaffirming that you are doing things right.

This is not a book of advanced techniques or secret, magical moves. It is a collection of around 150 solid training drills which we hope you are already well aware of. You will be able to use this book to crystallise your thoughts on each of the techniques - what works, what doesn't and why.

Such attention can only be of benefit to your students and while you may not agree with all of the techniques, or maybe you have a different take on them, the drills in the book are practiced by real stadium champions in Bangkok, Thailand. These are the training techniques that are bringing success.

By supplementing with your own, coaches notes, you can use the book as a working record of techniques covered, as a reference for grading or as a simple memory aid for Thai names.

Muay Thai Students and Fighters

This book helps your gym training by organising techniques and giving you a reference point to judge your Muay Thai progress.

When you get home from your training session, go through the book and find the techniques you just covered. Write in your notes while the memory is still fresh.

Before long, you will have built for yourself your very own personalised manual which will be of immense help to you as you progress in your own Muay Thai journey.

MMA and general martial arts enthusiasts

If you are interested in the martial arts in general, or especially if you practice MMA, this book will show you how Muay Thai power is generated through genuine, undiluted training routines, as used by current Muay Thai champions in Bangkok, Thailand.

While you may adapt the techniques to suit your own requirements, by training using the methods illustrated in this book you will gain a proper grounding in Muay Thai, direct from the source.

As a practical, easy to follow guide to genuine Muay Thai training, as practiced by the world's best, this book cannot be beaten.

Contents

With Pad Man *(continued)*

Bonus

Thai pronunciation: Mahd Trong

Notes: Thai style 1-2 gains its power by coordinating body rotation with footwork. The left foot lands with the jab and the right foot lands with the cross.

Your Notes

1-2 Hook

 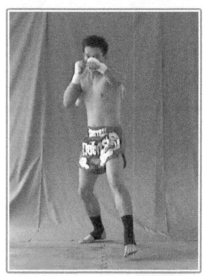

Notes: 1 (jab) lands with left foot, 2 (cross) lands with right foot and the hook requires full body rotation - note the left foot position in the final image.

Your Notes

Block Left Inside

Thai pronunciation: Yok Bang Nai Sai

Notes: Requires balance and a little flexibility. Note the fighter raises to the balls of his feet in the moment of blocking.

Your Notes

Block Left Outside

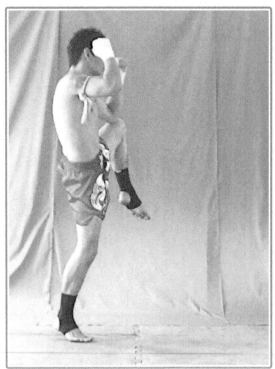 

Thai pronunciation: Yok Bang Sai

Notes: A strong block able to absorb the opponents rear round kick. Keep the arms in their original guard position and raise the knee to the elbow, creating no gap for the kick to pass through.

Your Notes

Block Right Inside

Thai pronunciation: Yok Bang Nai Kwa

Notes: As with the left inside block, good balance is needed. Do not twist the upper body (only the hips) else you will be left in a poor position to counter.

Your Notes

Block Right Outside

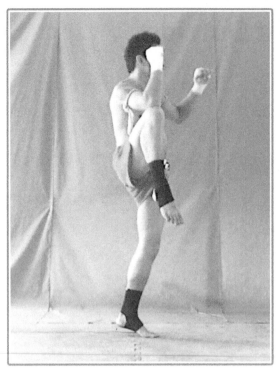 

Thai pronunciation: Yok Bang Kwa

Notes: As with the outside left block, extra control is gained by raising onto the ball of the standing leg. Lift the knee to the elbow to create a continuous wall of defence with no gaps.

Your Notes

Chop Elbow

Notes: Sink into the move to add extra body weight to the strike.

Your Notes

14

Cut Elbow

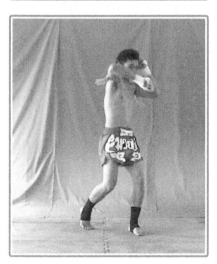 

Thai pronunciation: Sawk Dtahd

Notes: Horizontal rear elbow. Power comes from body rotation - note the hips twisting.

Your Notes

16

Elbow Hit

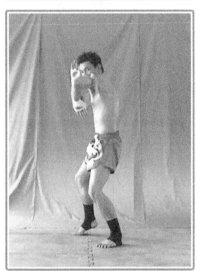 

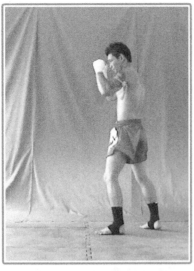 

Thai pronunciation: Sawk Dtee

Notes: Downwards lead elbow.   Use gravity (your body weight) for maximum power.

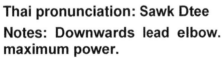

Your Notes

Flying Knee

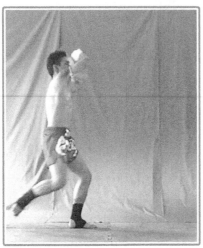 

Thai pronunciation: Kao Loi

Notes: A powerful technique, best used when the opponent is coming towards you, or has his movement restricted i.e. while he is in the corner.

Your Notes

Front Push Kick

Thai pronunciation: Teep Trong

Notes: Extend the hips to gain power. The action should be smooth throughout.

Your Notes

Jab

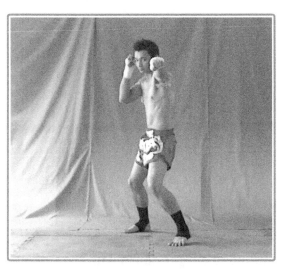 

Thai pronunciation: Mahd Trong

Notes: Drive off of the rear leg for power and keep a tight guard with the right hand.

Your Notes

Lever Up

Thai pronunciation: Sawk Gratung

Notes: A lesser used elbow technique. Can catch your opponent by surprise.

Your Notes

26

Reverse Elbow

 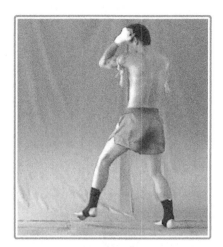

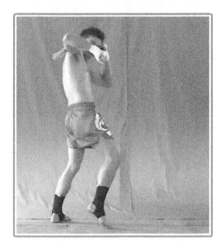 

Thai pronunciation: Sawk Glab

Notes: A beautiful and very effective technique. Lots of practice needed to judge distance.

Your Notes

Right Left Right

Notes: A great routine for practising body rotation and footwork coordination and guard.

Your Notes

Side Knee

Thai pronunciation: Kao Chiang

Notes: Similar in execution to the Thai round kick. Full hip rotation provides power.

Your Notes

Side Push Kick

Thai pronunciation: Teep Khang

Notes: A lot of distance can be covered with this technique.

Your Notes

Spear Elbow

Thai pronunciation: Sawk Pung

Notes: Similar to Lever Up elbow but with a horizontal attack angle.

Your Notes

Straight Kick

Thai pronunciation: Dteh Trong

Notes: Delivered as a snap kick by straightening the leg, rather than pushing with the hips. Target areas are the groin, abdomen, solar plexus, throat, under the chin or in the face. Pull back the toes to strike with the ball of the foot, or with greater flexibility, the heel may be used. Speed and accuracy are most important with this technique. When perfected, it is possible to strike for the eyes, using your toes.

Your Notes

Straight Knee

Thai pronunciation: Kao Trong

Notes: Deliver the knee smoothly, extending the hips and leaning far back to preserve balance and avoid a counter punch or elbow.

Your Notes

Thai Round Kick

Thai pronunciation: Dteh Lamtoa

Notes: Much has been written about this kick. Study these images carefully and practice, practice, practice. It is important to keep balance throughout.

Your Notes

Uppercut Elbow

Thai pronunciation: Sawk Nghad

Notes: Do not simply lift the elbow - drive it up using your thigh and calf muscles. Note how the fighter raises to the balls of his feet at the moment of impact.

Your Notes

Whipping Round Kick

Thai pronunciation: Dteh Dtahwad

Notes: This kick is a transition from a fake kick into real kick. By whipping the kick, the timing of the kick changes, confusing the opponent. Some power is lost as a result but with practice, this can still be a KO technique, especially when targeted at the jaw. Good hip flexibility is needed but practising the technique is a great way to achieve this. Contact point is the instep (top of the foot).

Your Notes

Arm Lock - Jab Counter

Thai pronunciation: Salab Fan Bplah

Notes: An older style technique but still effective once mastered.

Your Notes

Body Elbow - Cross Counter

Thai pronunciation: Paksa Waek Rang

Notes: Sink down and drive deep into the opponents guard. Target the solar plexus (centre of the chest) with full body rotation.

Your Notes

Body Elbow - Jab Counter

Thai pronunciation: Chawa Sad Hok

**Notes: Similar to the Body Elbow - Cross Counter (Paksa Waek Rang),
except that now you are striking at the opponents side/floating ribs.**

Your Notes

Body Punch to Lead Knee

Notes: A simple footstep between the punch and the knee provides the Thai power. You will be very close to your opponent after this combo so be prepared to capitalise on better clinch position or elbow opportunities.

Your Notes

Break and Knee - Clinch Counter

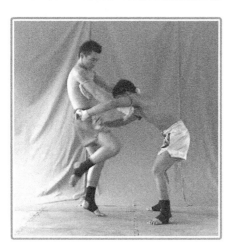 

Notes: A step back with the rear leg provides extra leverage and prepares you to deliver the knee strike.

Your Notes

Break Low Clinch

Notes: Pushing your opponents hips away creates a gap, down which you can push your hand. Execute these moves simultaneously to achieve best effect.

Your Notes

Catch and Body Punch - Kick Counter

Notes: Drive down and with full body rotation to deliver maximum power.

Your Notes

Catch and Elbow - Kick Counter

Notes: Target the face, collarbone or solar plexus. Release the opponents
leg to help close the distance.

Your Notes

Catch Push Reverse Elbow - Kick Counter

Thai pronunciation: Hiran Muan Paen Din

Notes: Push down on the opponents leg as you turn to upset his balance.

Your Notes

Catch Swap Sweep - Kick Counter

Notes: Much repetition is needed for you to apply this technique quickly. Use your free arm to help your opponent to the ground, pushing down while you kick upwards to his standing leg.

Your Notes

Catch Sweep - Kick Counter

Notes: This is a tough technique, clashing shin on shin. The advantage over kicking the back of your opponents leg is that he will tend to land face down on the ground, rather than on his back. Shin guards are essential when training this technique using full power.

Your Notes

Catch Throw - Side Knee Counter

Notes: Pull your body away from the knee strike to reduce impact and push down with your right hand to maximise the force of your opponents landing.

Your Notes

Clinch Lock and Straight Knee

 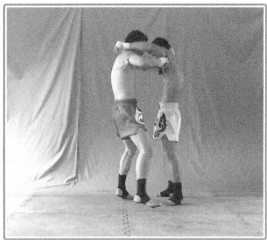

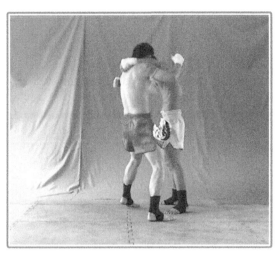 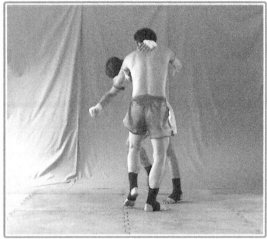

Thai pronunciation: Jab Nai Tee Trong

Notes: This move involves pulling with the left hand while stepping back with the left foot. This leaves you in an excellent position to deliver the left knee strike.

Your Notes

Clinch Outside to Inside

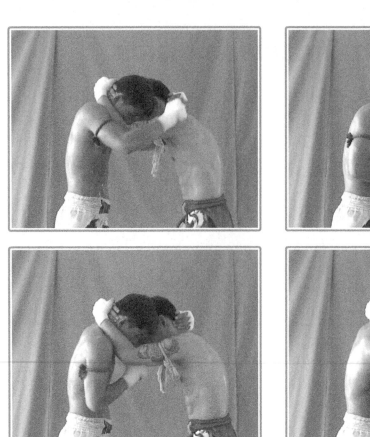

Thai pronunciation: Jan Nai

**Notes: This swapping of hand positions appears simple at first sight.
However, it should be practised often and with a variety of training partners
in order to understand the subtleties involved.**

Your Notes

Cross Catch to Jump Kick - Kick Counter

Notes: An unusual catch. After absorbing the kick with your right shoulder and forearm, your left hand scoops under to catch the opponents leg. You should pull the opponent towards you as you launch the jump kick.

Your Notes

Elbow - Knee Counter

Notes: Notice how the fighter delivering the elbow takes a step forward to further reduce the distance.

Your Notes

Elbow Chest Spike - Punch Counter

Thai pronunciation: Sak Phuang Malai

Notes: Keep a very tight guard as you enter for this technique. Be ready for a knee counter.

Your Notes

Elbow Leg Spike - Kick Counter

Thai pronunciation: Hak Nguang Aiyara

Notes: Rotate shoulders in a full circle for power and keep hold of the opponents leg after this move to keep many combination options open.

Your Notes

Elbow Shoulder Spike - Punch Counter

Thai pronunciation: Hong Pee Hak

Notes: Step in to close the distance and allow hip rotation for power.

Your Notes

Evade to Knee - Inside Leg Kick Counter

Notes: Move the lead leg back without shifting your bodyweight or upper body position else you will be too far away to deliver the counter knee.

Your Notes

Face Elbow - Jab Counter

Thai pronunciation: Ta Then Kham Fak

Notes: Step in deep to cover the distance.

Your Notes

Fake Lead Fake Rear to Lead Knee

Notes: A great technique for closing the distance to your opponent.

Your Notes

Fake Lead Knee to Rear Knee

Notes: Faking a knee confuses your opponent, making it much easier to land the real knee on target.

Your Notes

Front Kick to Face

Thai pronunciation: Batha Loob Pak

Notes: For maximum impact, time this move for when your opponent is stepping towards you.

Your Notes

Hand Down Kick

Notes: This is a controversial move. Most competition rules require that no part of the fighters body, other than his feet, are in contact with the ground.

Your Notes

Jab - Jab Counter

Thai pronunciation: Dab Chawala

Notes: A classic boxing counter. Notice how the Thai fighter steps in with his left foot to deliver his counter jab with maximum force. You will need to be able to 'read' your opponents intention to execute this technique well.

Your Notes

Jump Spin Kick - Evasion Counter

Notes: The coordination of the second round kick is quite different from other kicks in that the fighter launches from his right foot to deliver the right kick. The left foot also leaves the ground. Power is achieved by carrying the rotational momentum through from the first kick.

Your Notes

Jumping Scissor Knee

Notes: This move confuses the opponent, making him think the first knee is the intended move. In effect, this is a fake knee to real knee - all in the air.

Your Notes

Knee and Turn - Kick Counter

Notes: When turning your opponent, pull down (towards the ground) as well as around. Keep your right elbow low and use bodyweight rather than muscle. In case the opponent does not fall down, be prepared to follow with more knee strikes or kicks (see last image).

Your Notes

Left Hook - Left Kick Counter

Notes: Step towards the opponent to close distance and slightly to the left to reduce the impact of his kick. The punch is delivered using body rotation rather than swinging the arm. Note hip and shoulder position in last image.

Your Notes

Leg Check Twist Throw

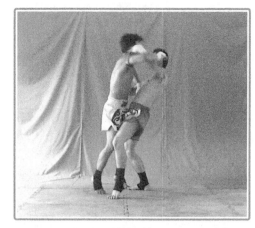

Notes: With your leg on the outside, pull the opponent towards you and twist, keeping your hips forward and your leg in its original position. The opponents thigh will be blocked by your thigh and he will start to fall. It is most important to move your blocking thigh away from the action as soon as you feel the opponent falling.

Your Notes

Leg Push Twist Throw

Notes: This throw involves pushing away with your thigh against your opponents thigh, while pulling his upper body towards you with the opposite hand.

Your Notes

Lock and Knee - Cross Counter

Thai pronunciation: Noo Tai Rao

Notes: Timing is crucial as you will need to read your opponents intention in order to step in and execute this classic Thai move effectively.

Your Notes

Outside Block - Kick Defence

 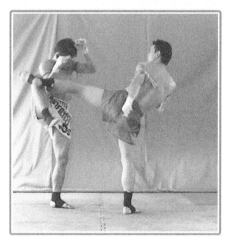

Notes: The objective is to absorb your opponents power without losing your own balance or position. Excellent control is needed to practice this block without the use of shin protection.

Your Notes

Outside Foot Sweep

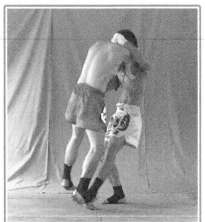 

Notes: Be sure to cleanly kick your opponents foot away, rather than tripping him by simply pulling him over your foot

Your Notes

98

Parry and Kick - Push Kick Counter

Notes: Do not move back as you parry, else you will be out of range for the following kick.

Your Notes

Parry and Knee - Push Kick Counter

Notes: It is vital to keep your bodyweight forward during the parry in order to maintain close proximity for the knee strike. In this picture sequence, the fighter delivers an extra kick at the end.

Your Notes

Push Kick - Round Kick Counter

Thai pronunciation: Mon Yan Laki

Notes: A simple and effective technique requiring good speed and timing. Very little power is needed.

Your Notes

Reverse Heel Kick - Evasion Counter

Notes: A spectacular and powerful technique. Striking point is the heel of the foot.

Your Notes

Side Kick - Evasion Counter

Thai pronunciation: Kwang Liew Lang

Notes: A very useful counter that will save you from trouble when your round kick misses.

Your Notes

Standing Leg Check - Kick Counter

Thai pronunciation: Grisorn Kham Huai

Notes: Speed, timing and accuracy are all more important than power with this surprisingly effective technique.

Your Notes

Step Catch Throw - Knee Counter

Thai pronunciation: Kanghan Tong Lom

Notes: An ancient and seldom seen technique.

Your Notes

Step-Up Elbow

Notes: After the climb, time the strike to land as your bodyweight is falling. The left hand position is important to maintain balance.

Your Notes

Step-Up Rear Kick

Notes: A spectacular kick that will please the audience.

Your Notes

Swapping Kicks

Notes: Much repetition leads to improved timing, distance and control.

Your Notes

Sweep - Kick Defence

Thai pronunciation: Then Klad Lan

Notes: As your opponent steps into his kick, so you should also step in the same direction. The larger your step, the better as it will reduce the force of your opponents kick and add power to your own

Your Notes

Swinging Side Knee

Notes: Throw your leg out straight behind you, allowing your hips to turn. Then swing your hips back and bend your leg at the knee, using momentum to deliver a more powerful strike.

Your Notes

Take Guard and Lead Elbow

Notes: Use your bodyweight to deliver maximum downward force and simply swipe away your opponents guard on the way.

Your Notes

Take Guard and Rear Elbow

Notes: Similar to 'Take Guard and Lead Elbow' except that more body rotation is used to deliver Thai power. Note the shoulder position in the last image.

Your Notes

Throw - Jumping Knee Defence

Notes: Twist your opponents body in the same direction that he is aiming his knee and he will fall quite easily. Start the twist as soon as possible to take advantage of your opponents momentum.

Your Notes

Turn and Knee 1

Notes: First step is towards your opponent (image 2). Second step is backwards and round, while pulling on your opponents neck. This gives extra leverage to the pull and prepares you to deliver the knee strike.

Your Notes

Turn and Knee 2

Notes: In this example, the fighter takes advantage of his opponents raised leg position (knee strike), pulling strongly down with his right hand while pushing up with his left forearm.

Your Notes

Turn and Knee 3

Notes: The fighter pushes with his left hand rather than pulling with his right. The strength for the push comes from the footwork, allowing full body rotation.

Your Notes

Twist Throw - Side Knee Counter

Notes: A simple backwards step (see image 2) allows you to increase the twist. Pull with one hand while pushing with the other.

Your Notes

Uppercut - Punch Counter

Thai pronunciation: Erawan Suey Nga

Notes: Shoulder rotation starts the move and power is enhanced by driving up with the hips. Note how the right hip is forward in the last image.

Your Notes

1-2 Left Kick Left Knee

Notes: The fighter makes a split-step (images 3 and 4) to improve the power of his left kick by making it his rear while keeping the same range. Note how the fighter ends the routine in opposite stance, with his right foot forwards.

Your Notes

1-2 Left Knee

Notes: A strong step into the knee (images 3 and 4) provides power.

Your Notes

1-2 Right Kick Right Knee

Notes: A fundamental drill using the fighters strongest weapons. Remember to step into the knee strike (image 9) to close distance and add power.

Your Notes

1-2 Slip Hook

Notes: Recoil from the slip position to deliver a devastatingly powerful left hook. Note the extremes of whole body rotation between images 4, 5 and 6.

Your Notes

Arm Block and Kick

Notes: Here, the padman tests the fighters stability before the kicks by striking heavily with the pads.

Your Notes

Block and Kick

Notes: Go for maximum power and speed with this drill.

Your Notes

Block Evade Right Knee

Notes: A marvellous drill involving blocking, evading and attacking.

Your Notes

Block Step Knee

Notes: A basic and fundamental drill. The fighter switches from block to attack in mid-move. This should be practised until it is automatic.

Your Notes

Block to Knee to Knee to Elbow

Notes: A more complicated drill that really tests the fighters footwork and distance.

Your Notes

Block to Sweep

Notes: Excellent control is needed with the sweep in order to not abuse your padman.

Your Notes

Blocking Drill

**Notes: This drill tests the fighters inside and outside block to both sides.
This is an essential drill which all fighters should master.**

Your Notes

Catch and Jump Knee

Notes: The fighter throws the padmans leg to the side before launching the knee. This drill uses lots of energy and is a lot of fun.

Your Notes

Catch and Kick

Notes: Step to the right when catching the padmans kick, then step back again to the left to deliver your own kick with maximum power. Notice the full body rotation between images 4, 5 and 6.

Your Notes

Catch and Knee

Notes: Step to the right when catching the padmans kick, then step forward to deliver the knee strike with power. Notice the fighters right hand coming forwards to act as guard. It is also effective to hold the pad man's neck down, pulling him into the knee.

Your Notes

Catch and Sweep

Notes: In this drill, the fighter catches the padmans Front Push Kick in his left hand. The right hand is used to control the padmans foot, preventing him from pulling his leg free. The fighter then feeds the leg under his left side before executing the sweep. The fighters right arm helps the padman fall.

Your Notes

Catch Hook to Elbow to Knee Drill

**Notes: A more advanced drill joining techniques in quick succession.
Practice this on both the left and the right sides, as illustrated above.**

Your Notes

Catch Hook to Knee

Notes: Make sure to practice this on both the left and right sides and remember to pull the padman down into the knee to increase the impact.

Your Notes

Clinch Right Knee to Left Knee

Notes: This drill can be cycled over and again. Notice the footwork and how the fighter makes a strong, positive step into each knee strike without skipping or split-stepping.

Your Notes

Collapse Kick to Knee

Notes: The fighter positions his heel into the gap under the padmans armpit (image 5) then uses bodyweight to push down and release his leg.

Your Notes

Cross Block to Lead Kick

Notes: The challenge here is to not lose balance or position during the block, else you will not be able to perform the following kick. Notice the minimal footwork.

Your Notes

Cross Block to Spin Up Elbow

Notes: There are only two footsteps in this drill. You will need to place your feet perfectly to accomplish this technique.

Your Notes

Elbow Drill 1

Notes: The fighter returns to guard position between each elbow.

Your Notes

Elbow Drill 2

Notes: Drive upwards with the whole body at the point of impact, using thigh and calf muscles as well as hip rotation. Notice the hip position in images 3 and 6.

Your Notes

Elbow Drill 3

Notes: As with all repetitive padwork drills, it is vital to maintain an effective guard.

Your Notes

Evade and Left Kick - Inside Leg Kick Counter

Notes: The padman may kick with full speed to truly test the fighters counter.

Your Notes

Evade and Left Kick and Left Knee

Notes: The distance is slightly reduced between the kick and the knee. Consider images 7 and 12.

Your Notes

Evade to Right Cross to Right Knee

Notes: The range between the fighter and the padman is almost identical for both the cross punch and the knee.

Your Notes

Face Elbow - Cross Counter

Notes: A simple yet powerful technique where the fighter steps in at the same time as the padman throws the cross.

Your Notes

Fake Lead Knee to Rear Elbow

Notes: The fighters rear foot comes forward with the elbow strike (image 6).

Your Notes

Fake Lead Knee to Rear Kick

Notes: The fighter turns his foot (image 4) in readiness for the kick.

Your Notes

Fake Lead Knee to Rear Knee

Notes: The fighter returns to his original position in the final image. Notice the large distance between him and his padman.

Your Notes

Fake Rear Knee to Lead Elbow

Notes: The fake knee increases the fighters chances of landing the powerful elbow strike by confusing the opponent. Make the fake knee as realistic as possible.

Your Notes

Fake Rear Knee to Lead Kick

Notes: The fake rear knee allows the fighter to take a large step forward while putting the opponent on the defence.

Your Notes

Fake Round Kick to Push Kick

Notes: A simple and effective fake move. With a little luck, the opponent will attempt to block the fake round kick and be left standing on one foot when you deliver the true push kick.

Your Notes

Flying Knee

Notes: Thrust the hips forward at the moment of strike. Note how the padman uses both pads to absorb the powerful impact.

Your Notes

Hook to Elbow to Double Knee

Notes: Though a right knee may feel more natural after the right elbow, the left knee is more unexpected and therefore more likely to land. Note the fighter steps into the knee rather than skipping or split-stepping.

Your Notes

Hook to Elbow to Skip Knee

Notes: The skip allows the fighter to change leg stance without changing the distance to the target. The fighter is weak while skipping this way so the move is made quickly and without jumping up.

Your Notes

Jab to Body Shot to Hook to Low Kick

Notes: This combination focuses on striking high, low, high, low.

Your Notes

Jab to Left Low Kick to Left Mid Kick

Notes: Care should be taken to control the inside low kick, delivering it with speed but with no power, followed by maximum power with the left kick to the pads. Look after your padman.

Your Notes

Jab to Right Low Kick to Right Mid Kick

Notes: In this sequence, the padman is in a southpaw stance. The combination works just the same with the padman in an orthodox stance, this time striking to the padmans outer thigh.

Your Notes

Jumping Rear Elbow

Notes: The fighters left hand comes forward (images 2, 3 and 4) to act as a guard and to gauge distance to the target.

Your Notes

Lead Push Kick to Rear Knee

Notes: After the push kick, the fighters left foot is placed immediately in position for the right knee. There is only one footstep in this combination.

Your Notes

Lead Push Kick to Rear Low Kick

Notes: A single step combination. After the push kick, the fighter must judge where to place his left foot, depending on where the padman has been pushed.

Your Notes

Lean Back and Left Kick

Notes: In this sequence, the fighter skips into the left kick to maintain his range. During your padwork sessions, you should encourage your padman to throw high kicks at random times so you can make this move become an automatic response.

Your Notes

185

Lean Back and Right Kick

Notes: A small step back with your rear leg widens your base and lets you lean back further. Be careful not to take too large a step back else you will be out of range for the kick.

Your Notes

Left Elbow Right Knee

Notes: A nice training combination that should feel natural. Make sure to add a step when delivering the knee (image 4). This step allows for small adjustments to range and adds Thai power to the knee strike.

Your Notes

Left Push Kick

Notes: There are no footsteps in this drill. The fighter simply raises his lead, left leg, executes the push kick, then returns his foot to its starting position. This is a deceptively difficult technique as most fighters will want to move their right foot forwards prior to the push kick. Practice makes perfect.

Your Notes

Lever Up

Notes: This drill uses the Lever Up elbow as a cross counter. Make sure your padman is ready and expecting your strike.

Your Notes

Parry and Knee - Cross Counter

Notes: Pull the padman into the knee with your right arm to increase the power of this classic Thai technique.

Your Notes

Parry and Knee - Jab Counter

Notes: Note how the fighter steps forward with his right foot while reaching out with his left hand (images 4 and 5). This is not a complicated technique but it does require some practice.

Your Notes

Parry and Left Kick - Push Kick Counter

Notes: Maintain your foot position during the parry. Note how the fighter steps slightly to his right before delivering the left kick in order to increase its power.

Your Notes

Parry and Left Kick - Push Kick Counter

Notes: In this sequence, the fighter is slightly out of stance during the parry and has to adjust by making a step forwards to deliver the kick (image 3).

Your Notes

Parry to Low Kick

Notes: Step into the kick while completing the parry (image 4). Remember, be nice to your padman. Control, control, control.

Your Notes

Push Block Drill

Notes: The object of this drill is to maintain stance and balance and to improve accuracy and timing. All you need do is stop the padmans kick by placing your foot in the way of his thigh. Practice will teach you the correct timing and foot placement.

Your Notes

Push Kick Drill

Notes: With this drill, you are reacting to the padmans whole bodyweight coming forward. Timing is improved as well as balance. You will need to feel the padmans momentum as your push kick lands and adjust your power accordingly. Too little power will see you pushed backwards, too much and you will be forced to step forward, losing your stance and position.

Your Notes

Push Kick to Knee to Turn to Knee

Notes: A good drill that includes changing range and position. Pay close attention to the footwork.

Your Notes

Rear Round Kick to Lead Push Kick

Notes: Practical and realistic, this is a drill that should be mastered.

Your Notes

Reverse Elbow

Notes: This spinning, or reverse elbow is covered elsewhere in this book. Here, we can see how the fighter returns to stance, turning back the same way rather than turning full circle.

Your Notes

Right Elbow Left Knee

Notes: Here we can see the fighter skipping into opposite stance (image 4) in order to maintain the same range while making his left knee into a stronger, rear knee.

Your Notes

Right Left Right

Notes: Study the shoulder, hip and foot positions during this basic yet fundamental punching drill.

Your Notes

Side Push Kick

Notes: The Thai 'belly pad' is an essential piece of equipment to practice this technique with full power.

Your Notes

Swinging Right Knee

Notes: In this example, the padman is using small focus mitts. This requires a high degree of accuracy and control from both the padman and fighter.

Your Notes

Take Guard and Lead Elbow

Notes: Taking the guard away and delivering the elbow are carried out as one smooth, continuous move. Power drives from the rear leg. Note how the Thai pad nearly folds in two with the power of the strike in the final image.

Your Notes

Take Guard and Rear Elbow

Notes: The footwork is subtle but can be seen in image 4 where the fighter moves closer to the target. This elbow is delivered horizontally using body rotation and the rear leg for power. Note the shoulder, hip and rear foot position in the final image.

Your Notes

Turn and Left Knee

Notes: Two steps round to turn the padman are followed by one step forwards to deliver power to the knee strike. As always, pull the padman down into the knee to increase the impact.

Your Notes

Turn and Right Knee

Notes: The footwork and general positioning is displayed well in this image sequence. Remember to make an extra step (image 6) before delivering the knee strike.

Your Notes

Uppercut - Hook - Cross

Notes: A footstep occurs as each punch is landed. This is fundamental to delivering Thai power to the strikes. Right foot lands with the right uppercut, left foot with the left hook and right foot again with the final right cross. These steps allow the hips and shoulders to more fully rotate

Your Notes

1-2 - Tyre Rhythm

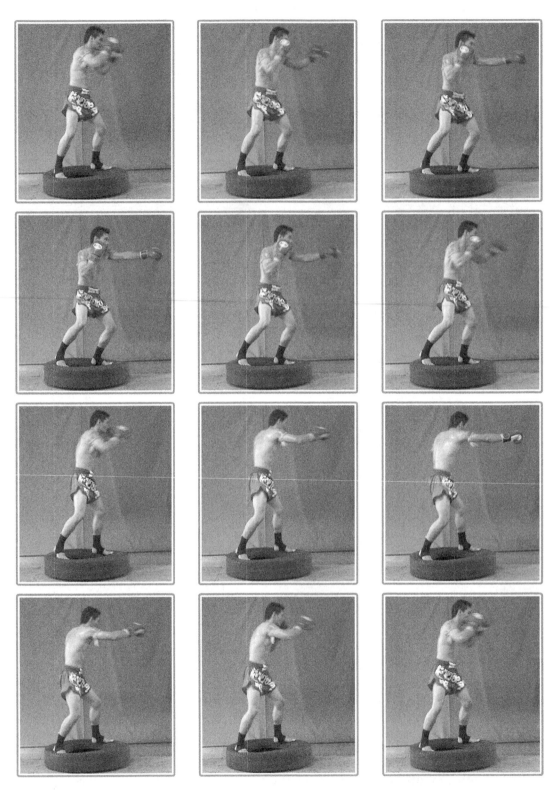

Notes: Weight moves to the front leg with the jab and to the back leg with the cross. Study these images closely to see the tyre respond.

Your Notes

Your Notes

Made in the USA
Las Vegas, NV
06 February 2022

43321873R00125